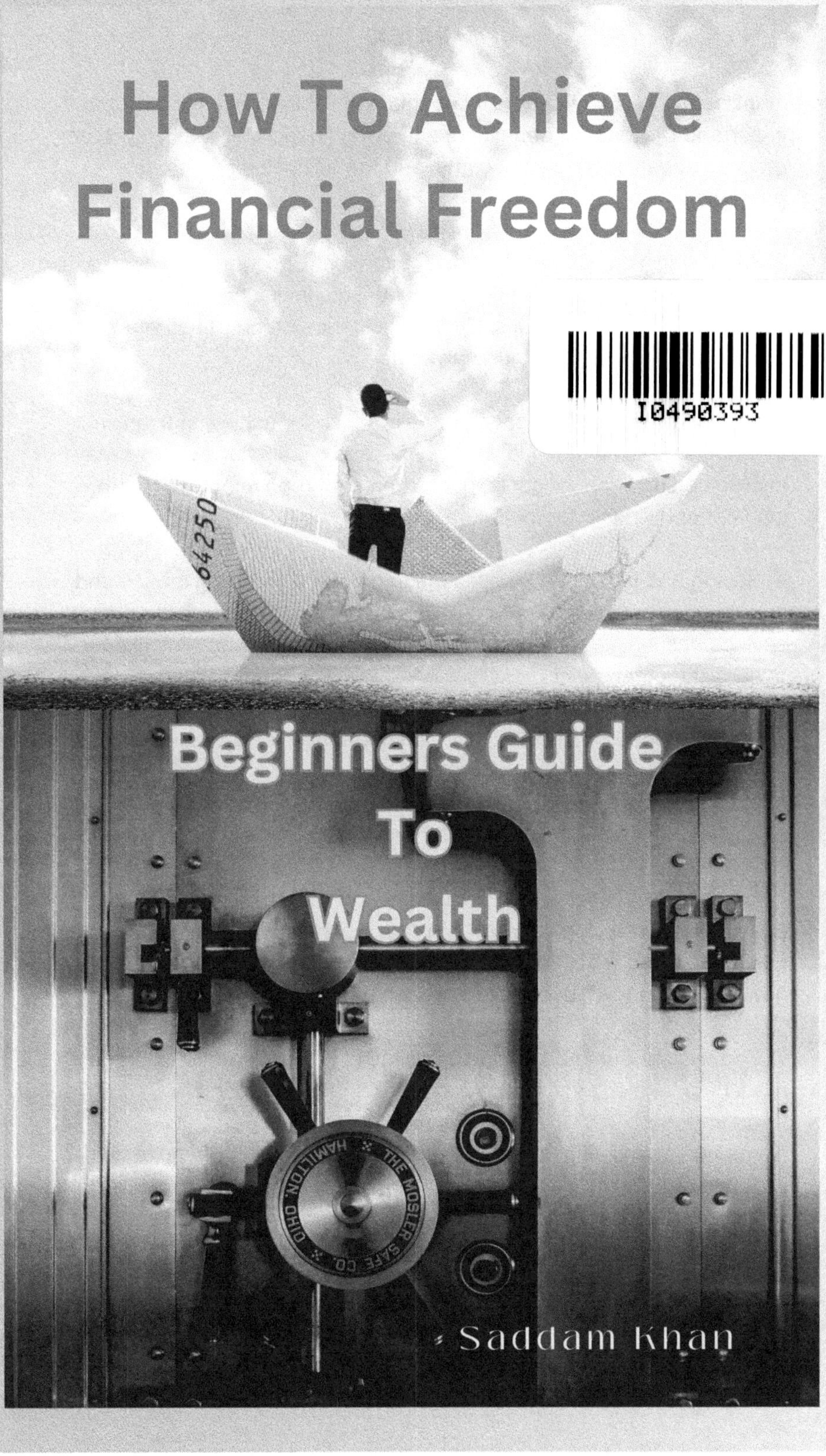

How To Achieve Financial Freedom

Beginners Guide To Wealth

Saddam Khan

INDEX

1. Introduction: Explain the concept of financial freedom and why it is important. Discuss the benefits of achieving financial freedom, such as reduced stress, increased security, and the ability to pursue one's passions.

2. Assessing Your Current Financial Situation: Encourage readers to take a close look at their current financial situation, including their income, expenses, debt, and savings. Provide guidance on how to create a budget, track expenses, and analyze debt.

3. Creating a Plan: Help readers create a plan for achieving financial freedom, based on their individual goals and circumstances. This may involve setting financial goals, prioritizing debt repayment, increasing income, or investing for the future.

4. Saving and Investing: Discuss the importance of saving money and investing for the future. Provide guidance on how to choose the best savings accounts, create an emergency fund, and invest in stocks, bonds, and other assets.

5. Building Good Habits: Discuss the importance of building good financial habits, such as avoiding debt, living below one's means, and avoiding impulse purchases. Provide tips for staying motivated and disciplined in the pursuit of financial freedom.

6. Overcoming Obstacles: Acknowledge the obstacles that can prevent people from achieving financial freedom, such as lack of discipline, unexpected expenses, and economic downturns. Provide guidance on how to stay on track despite these obstacles.

7. Conclusion: Summarize the key points of the book and encourage readers to take action towards achieving financial freedom.

Remember, achieving financial freedom is a journey that requires time, patience, and discipline. By following the steps outlined in this ebook, readers can take control of their finances and work towards a life of financial security and independence.

Introduction

Financial freedom is the ability to live a comfortable life without worrying about money. It is the state of being in control of one's finances and having enough resources to meet all of one's needs and wants. Achieving financial freedom can provide numerous benefits, including reduced stress, increased security, and the ability to pursue one's passions.

Financial stress can have a significant impact on one's mental and physical health. Constant worry about money can lead to anxiety, depression, and even physical health problems. Achieving financial freedom can help reduce this stress and improve one's overall well-being.

Financial freedom also provides increased security. With a solid financial plan in place, individuals can better protect themselves and their families from unexpected emergencies and financial setbacks. They can also better plan for the future and ensure that they are prepared for retirement.

Finally, achieving financial freedom can provide the ability to pursue one's passions. When individuals are no longer burdened by financial stress, they can explore new interests, travel, or pursue hobbies that they may not have had the time or resources to do before.

In conclusion, financial freedom is an important concept that can provide numerous benefits to individuals and their families. By taking control of their finances and creating a solid financial plan, individuals can reduce stress, increase security, and pursue their passions.

Assessing your current financial situation

Assessing your current financial situation is a critical step toward achieving financial freedom. It requires a deep understanding of your income, expenses, debt, and savings. Here are some tips to help you assess your current financial situation:

1. Calculate your income
2. Track your expenses
3. Analyze your debt
4. Review your savings
5. Create a budget
6. Analyze your debt
7. Increase your savings

By assessing your current financial situation and creating a solid financial plan, you can take control of your finances and work towards achieving financial freedom. Remember to track your progress and adjust your plan as needed to stay on track toward your goals.

1. **Calculate your income**: Determine your total income from all sources, including your salary, side hustle income, investment income, and any other sources of income. To calculate your income, you need to add up all sources of income. Here are some examples of income sources to consider:
1. Salary or wages from your job.
2. Side hustle income, such as income from freelance work, part-time jobs, or selling items online.
3. Investment income, such as dividends or capital gains from stocks, mutual funds, or real estate investments.
4. Rental income, if you own rental property.
5. Social Security income, if you are retired or disabled.
6. Pension income, if you receive a pension from your employer.

Add up all of these sources of income to determine your total income. Make sure to consider all income sources, including those that may not come in regularly or that may be seasonal.

This will give you an accurate picture of your overall income and help you create a realistic budget.

2. **Track your expenses**: Keep track of all your expenses for at least a month, including your bills, food, transportation, entertainment, and any other expenses. Use a budgeting app or spreadsheet to help you stay organized. Tracking your expenses is essential to understanding your spending habits and identifying areas where you can cut back to save money. Here are some tips for tracking your expenses:

1. Start by creating a list of all your monthly expenses, including bills, rent or mortgage payments, food, transportation, and entertainment.

2. Keep track of all your expenses for at least a month by recording every transaction in a budgeting app, spreadsheet, or notebook.

3. Categorize your expenses into different categories, such as housing, utilities, food, transportation, entertainment, and miscellaneous.

4. Review your expenses regularly to identify areas where you can cut back or find ways to save money.

5. Use a budgeting app or spreadsheet to help you stay organized and track your progress toward your financial goals.

6. Be honest with yourself about your spending habits and be willing to make changes to achieve your financial goals.

By tracking your expenses, you can identify areas where you may be overspending and find ways to cut back to save money. This can help you free up more money to pay down debt or increase your savings, bringing you closer to achieving financial freedom.

3. **Analyze your debt**: Make a list of all your debts, including credit card debt, student loans, car loans, and mortgages. Record the interest rate and monthly payment for each debt Analyzing your debt is an important step toward achieving financial freedom. Here are some tips for analyzing your debt:
   1. Make a list of all your debts, including credit card debt, student loans, car loans, and mortgages.

2. Record the interest rate, balance, and minimum monthly payment for each debt.
3. Prioritize your debts by interest rate, starting with the highest interest rate debt first.
4. Create a plan to pay off your debts by making extra payments towards the debt with the highest interest rate while making minimum payments on your other debts.
5. Consider debt consolidation or refinancing options to help reduce interest rates and make payments more manageable.
6. Once you pay off one debt, move on to the next highest interest rate debt and repeat the process until all of your debts are paid off.

By analyzing your debt and creating a plan to pay it off, you can reduce your financial stress and increase your financial security. Paying off debt also frees up more money to put towards savings and investments, bringing you closer to achieving financial freedom.

4. **Review your savings**: Determine how much you have saved in emergency funds, retirement accounts, and any other savings accounts. Reviewing your savings is an important step toward achieving financial freedom. Here are some tips for reviewing your savings:

1. Determine how much you have saved in emergency funds, retirement accounts, and any other savings accounts.
2. Evaluate whether you have enough saved in your emergency fund to cover at least 3-6 months of living expenses in case of an unexpected event, such as a job loss or medical emergency.
3. Review your retirement accounts, such as a 401(k) or IRA, and evaluate whether you are contributing enough to meet your retirement goals. Consider increasing your contributions if necessary.
4. Consider opening a separate savings account for specific goals, such as a down payment on a home or a vacation.
5. Evaluate whether your savings are earning a competitive interest rate. Consider switching to a higher interest-rate account if necessary.
6. Set specific savings goals and create a plan to achieve them. For example, if you want to save for a down payment on a home, determine how much you need to save each month and adjust your budget accordingly.

By reviewing your savings, you can ensure that you are on track to achieve your financial goals and increase your financial security. It also helps you identify areas where you may need to save more or adjust your savings strategy to better align with your goals.

5. **Create a budget:** Use your income, expenses, and debt to create a budget that works for you. Make sure to include all your monthly bills and expenses, as well as a plan to pay down your debts and increase your savings. Creating a budget is a crucial step toward achieving financial freedom. Here are some tips for creating a budget:
    1. Use your income, expenses, and debt to create a budget that works for you.
    2. Start by listing all your sources of income, including your salary, side hustle income, and investment income.
    3. Next, list all your expenses, including your bills, rent or mortgage payments, food, transportation, entertainment, and any other expenses.
    4. Categorize your expenses into different categories, such as housing, utilities, food, transportation, entertainment, and miscellaneous.
    5. Evaluate your expenses and identify areas where you can cut back to save money. For example, consider packing your lunch instead of eating out or using public transportation instead of driving.
    6. Make a plan to pay down your debts by allocating extra money towards the debt with the highest interest rate while making minimum payments on your other debts.
    7. Set savings goals and allocate money towards your emergency fund, retirement accounts, and any other savings accounts.
    8. Review your budget regularly and make adjustments as necessary to ensure that you are on track to achieve your financial goals.

By creating a budget, you can take control of your finances and make sure that you are living within your means. It also helps you identify areas where you can cut back to save money, pay down debt, and increase your savings, bringing you closer to achieving financial freedom.

6. **Analyze your debt:** Identify any high-interest debts and make a plan to pay them off as soon as possible. Consider debt consolidation or refinancing options to help reduce interest rates and make payments more manageable. Analyzing your debt is an important step toward achieving financial freedom. Here are some tips for analyzing and paying off your debt:
    1. Make a list of all your debts, including credit card debt, student loans, car loans, and mortgages.
    2. Record the interest rate and monthly payment for each debt.
    3. Identify any high-interest debts with interest rates above 6-8% and prioritize paying them off first.
    4. Consider debt consolidation or refinancing options to help reduce interest rates and make payments more manageable.

5. If you have multiple credit card debts, consider consolidating them into a single low-interest loan.
6. Make a plan to pay off your debts by allocating extra money towards the debt with the highest interest rate while making minimum payments on your other debts.
7. Consider using the snowball method, where you pay off the smallest debt first and then move on to the next smallest debt.
8. Consider earning extra income through a side hustle or part-time job to help pay off your debt faster.

By analyzing your debt and making a plan to pay it off, you can reduce your financial stress and increase your financial security. It also helps you identify areas where you can save money on interest payments and allocate more money toward achieving your financial goals.

7. **Increase your savings**: Find ways to increase your savings by cutting unnecessary expenses, increasing your income, or finding new investment opportunities Increasing your savings is an important step towards achieving financial freedom. Here are some tips for increasing your savings:

1. Cut unnecessary expenses: Review your budget and identify areas where you can cut back on expenses. Consider reducing your entertainment budget, eating out less frequently, or canceling subscriptions that you don't use.
2. Increase your income: Consider ways to increase your income, such as taking on a side hustle or part-time job, asking for a raise at your current job, or pursuing new career opportunities.
3. Find new investment opportunities: Look for new investment opportunities that can help you grow your savings over time. Consider investing in stocks, mutual funds, or real estate.
4. Automate your savings: Set up automatic transfers from your checking account to your savings account each month to ensure that you are consistently saving money.
5. Increase your retirement contributions: Increase your contributions to your employer-sponsored retirement plan or start an individual retirement account (IRA) to help you save for retirement.
6. Set savings goals: Set specific savings goals for yourself, such as saving for a down payment on a home or a vacation, and create a plan to achieve them.

By increasing your savings, you can build a strong financial foundation and achieve greater financial security. It also provides you with more options to pursue your passions and enjoy life on your own terms.

Creating a Plan

Creating a plan involves setting financial goals, prioritizing debt repayment, increasing income, or investing for the future.
Creating a plan is an essential step toward achieving financial freedom. Here are some tips for creating a plan that works for you:

1. Set financial goals
2. Prioritize debt repayment
3. Increase your income
4. Build an emergency fund
5. Create a budget
6. Automate your savings
7. Invest for the future

By creating a plan that is tailored to your individual goals and circumstances, you can take control of your finances and achieve financial freedom. It takes time, discipline, and patience, but with the right mindset and strategy, it is achievable.

1. **Setting financial goals**: Define your financial goals and objectives, such as saving for retirement, paying off debt, or buying a home. Make sure your goals are specific, measurable, and achievable within a realistic timeframe. Setting financial goals is a crucial step toward achieving financial freedom. Here are some tips for setting effective financial goals:

1. Be specific: Define your financial goals as precisely as possible. For example, instead of setting a vague goal of "saving money," set a specific goal such as "saving $10,000 for a down payment on a house."

2. Make them measurable: Create a measurable goal by establishing a specific dollar amount or percentage. This allows you to track your progress and determine when you have achieved your goal.

3. Set realistic timelines: Consider your income, expenses, and debt when setting timelines for your goals. Avoid setting unrealistic deadlines that may discourage you from pursuing your goals.

4. Prioritize your goals: Determine which goals are most important to you and prioritize them accordingly. For example, you may want to prioritize paying off high-interest debt before saving for a down payment on a house.

5. Break them down into smaller steps: Break down your goals into smaller, more manageable steps. This makes your goals feel more achievable and allows you to celebrate small victories along the way.

By setting specific, measurable, and achievable financial goals, you can create a roadmap for achieving financial freedom. Remember to regularly review and adjust your goals as needed to ensure you stay on track.

1. **Prioritize debt repayment**: Prioritize paying off your high-interest debts, such as credit card debt, student loans, or personal loans. Use the snowball or avalanche method to pay off your debts efficiently. Prioritizing debt repayment is an important step toward achieving financial freedom. Here are some tips for effectively paying off your debts:

1. Identify your debts: Make a list of all your debts, including the amount owed, interest rates, and minimum monthly payments.
2. Determine a strategy: Choose a debt repayment strategy that works best for you. Two popular methods are the snowball method and the avalanche method.
   - Snowball method: This method involves paying off your debts in order of smallest to largest balance, regardless of interest rate. This approach can help build momentum as you quickly pay off smaller debts and gain motivation to tackle larger debts.
   - Avalanche method: This method involves paying off your debts in order of highest to the lowest interest rate. This approach saves you more money in the long run by reducing the amount of interest you pay over time.
3. Cut expenses: Look for ways to cut expenses and free up extra money to put towards your debt payments. This could include reducing your spending on dining out, entertainment, or clothing.
4. Increase your income: Consider ways to increase your income, such as taking on a side hustle or negotiating a raise at work. Any extra money you make can be put towards paying off your debts.
5. Monitor your progress: Keep track of your progress by regularly checking your account balances and tracking your debt repayment goals. Celebrate your victories along the way and stay motivated to achieve your ultimate goal of financial freedom.

Paying off debt can take time and require discipline, but it's worth it in the long run. By prioritizing debt repayment and using an effective strategy, you can take control of your finances and work towards achieving financial freedom.

3. **Increase your income**: Consider ways to increase your income, such as taking on a side hustle or part-time job, starting a business, or pursuing a higher-paying career. Look for opportunities to earn passive income through investments or rental properties. Increasing your income is an essential step in achieving financial freedom. Here are some ways to increase your income:

1. Take on a side hustle or part-time job: Consider taking on a side job or part-time work to supplement your income. This could be anything from driving for a ride-share company to freelancing in your area of expertise.
2. Start a business: If you have an entrepreneurial spirit, consider starting your own business. This could be anything from an online store to a brick-and-mortar business. Be sure to research your market and competition, create a solid business plan, and secure funding as needed.
3. Pursue a higher-paying career: Look for opportunities to advance your career or switch to a higher-paying job. Consider pursuing additional education or certifications to qualify for higher-paying positions.
4. Earn passive income: Invest in stocks, real estate, or other investments that generate passive income. Rental properties, dividend-paying stocks, and index funds are all examples of investments that can provide passive income.
5. Monetize your hobbies: Look for ways to monetize your hobbies or skills. For example, if you enjoy photography, you could sell your photos online or offer your services as a photographer for events.

Increasing your income is a long-term strategy that requires effort and patience. It may take time to see the results, but with dedication and perseverance, you can work towards achieving financial freedom.

4. **Build an emergency fund**: Set aside funds in an emergency savings account to cover unexpected expenses or income interruptions. Aim for at least three to six months of living expenses. Building an emergency fund is an essential step in achieving financial freedom. Here are some tips to help you build your emergency fund:

1. Start small: Begin by setting aside a small amount of money each month, even if it's just a few dollars. Consistency is key, so make sure to contribute to your emergency fund regularly.

2. Cut expenses: Look for ways to cut your expenses and redirect that money into your emergency fund. Consider canceling subscriptions or memberships you no longer need, reducing your dining out or entertainment expenses, or finding more affordable ways to meet your needs.

3. Automate your savings: Set up automatic transfers from your checking account to your emergency savings account. This way, you won't have to remember to transfer money each month, and you'll be more likely to save consistently.

4. Consider a high-yield savings account: Look for a savings account that offers a higher interest rate than your regular savings account. This can help your emergency fund grow faster.

Building an emergency fund takes time and effort, but it's a crucial step in achieving financial freedom. With a solid emergency fund in place, you'll be better equipped to handle unexpected expenses or income interruptions without derailing your financial goals.

5. **Create a budget**: Create a realistic budget that incorporates your income, expenses, and debt repayments. Use a budgeting app or spreadsheet to help you stay organized and track your progress. Creating a budget is an important step in achieving financial freedom. Here are some tips to help you create a realistic budget:

1. Determine your income: Calculate your total monthly income, including your salary, side hustle income, and any other sources of income.
2. List your expenses: Make a list of all your monthly expenses, including fixed expenses like rent or mortgage payments, utilities, car payments, and insurance, as well as variable expenses like groceries, dining out, and entertainment.
3. Prioritize debt repayment: Prioritize paying off your high-interest debts, such as credit card debt, student loans, or personal loans. Use the snowball or avalanche method to pay off your debts efficiently.
4. Allocate savings: Set aside funds for your emergency fund and other savings goals, such as retirement or a down payment on a home.
5. Cut unnecessary expenses: Look for ways to cut your expenses, such as canceling subscriptions or memberships you no longer need, reducing your dining out or entertainment expenses, or finding more affordable ways to meet your needs.
6. Monitor your spending: Use a budgeting app or spreadsheet to track your spending and adjust your budget as needed.

A budget is a living document that should be regularly reviewed and updated as your financial situation changes. By creating a realistic budget and sticking to it, you'll be on your way to achieving financial freedom.

6. **Automate your savings**: Set up automatic transfers from your checking account to your savings account and retirement accounts each month. This ensures that you are consistently saving money and making progress toward your financial goals. Automating your savings can be a great way to stay on track with your financial goals.

 By setting up automatic transfers from your checking account to your savings account and retirement accounts, you can ensure that you're consistently putting money away without even having to think about it. This can help you build up your emergency fund, save for a down payment on a home, or invest for retirement. When setting up automatic transfers, be sure to consider your budget and make sure you have enough money in your checking account to cover your bills and other expenses. You can also consider automating your debt payments to ensure that you never miss a payment and avoid any late fees or penalties.

7. **Invest for the future**: Consider investing in stocks, bonds, mutual funds, or real estate to help you grow your wealth over time. Consult a financial advisor or do your own research to determine the best investment options for your goals and risk tolerance. Yes, investing can be an important part of achieving financial freedom. By investing for the long term, you can potentially grow your wealth and achieve your financial goals more quickly. When investing, it's important to consider your goals, risk tolerance, and time horizon. A financial advisor can help you create an investment plan that is tailored to your individual needs and circumstances. Alternatively, you can do your own research and learn about different investment options, such as stocks, bonds, mutual funds, or real estate.
Remember that investing always involves risk, so it's important to understand the potential risks and rewards before you invest. Diversification can also help reduce risk by spreading your investments across different asset classes and sectors. Ultimately, the key to successful investing is to have a long-term perspective and to stick to your plan even in times of market volatility.

Saving and Investing

In this chapter, we will discuss the importance of saving money and investing for the future. Here I will provide guidance on how to choose the best savings accounts, create an emergency fund, and invest in stocks, bonds, and other assets. Saving and investing are two important pillars of achieving financial freedom. While saving helps to build a financial cushion for emergencies, investing helps to grow your wealth over time. Here are some tips to help you save and invest effectively:

1. Choose the best savings accounts
2. Create an emergency fund
3. Set up automatic transfers
4. Invest in stocks, bonds, and other assets
5. Diversify your portfolio
6. Stay disciplined

Remember, saving and investing are long-term strategies that require patience, discipline, and consistency. With time, effort, and the right mindset, you can build a strong financial foundation and achieve financial freedom.

1. **Choose the best savings accounts**: Shop around to find the best savings accounts with high-interest rates and low fees. Consider online banks, which often offer higher rates than traditional brick-and-mortar banks. Also, look for accounts that are FDIC-insured for added security. Compare features such as minimum balance requirements, monthly maintenance fees, and ATM access to find an account that meets your needs.

   1. Consider investing in stocks: Investing in stocks can be a great way to grow your wealth over time, but it comes with risks. Research companies and industries that interest you, and invest in a diversified portfolio to minimize risk. Consider consulting a financial advisor to help you make investment decisions.
   2. Explore bonds and other fixed-income assets: Bonds and other fixed-income assets can provide a steady stream of income while also minimizing risk. Look for bonds with high credit ratings and diversify your portfolio with a mix of assets.
   3. Invest in real estate: Real estate can provide a steady stream of passive income through rental properties and also has the potential for appreciation over time. Consider investing in real estate investment trusts (REITs) or purchasing rental properties to add to your portfolio.

4. Rebalance your portfolio regularly: Regularly review and adjust your portfolio to ensure that it remains aligned with your financial goals and risk tolerance. Rebalancing can help you stay on track and avoid overexposure to certain assets.

2. **Create an emergency fund**: Aim to save at least three to six months of living expenses in an emergency fund. This will help you cover unexpected expenses, such as job loss, medical bills, or car repairs, without having to rely on credit cards or loans.
   1. Set a savings goal: Determine how much you want to save each month and set a goal for your emergency fund. You can use automated savings apps or create a separate savings account specifically for your emergency fund.
   2. Consider investing in a retirement account: If you have a retirement account available through your employer, such as a 401(k) or 403(b), make sure you are contributing enough to receive any employer match. You may also want to consider opening an Individual Retirement Account (IRA) to supplement your employer-sponsored plan.
   3. Understand the risks and rewards of investing: Investing in stocks, bonds, and other assets can help grow your wealth over time, but it also carries risks. Make sure you understand the potential risks and rewards before investing and consider consulting a financial advisor to help you make informed decisions.
   4. Diversify your investments: Diversification is key to minimizing risk in your investment portfolio. Consider investing in a mix of stocks, bonds, and other assets across different sectors and geographic regions.
   5. Regularly review and rebalance your portfolio: Review your investment portfolio regularly to ensure it aligns with your goals and risk tolerance. Consider rebalancing your portfolio periodically to maintain your desired asset allocation.

3. **Set up automatic transfers**: Make saving a habit by setting up automatic transfers from your checking account to your savings account each month. This ensures that you are consistently saving money and making progress toward your financial goals. Setting up automatic transfers is an easy way to make saving a habit and to ensure that you are saving money regularly.
You can set up automatic transfers through your bank's website or mobile app, and choose the amount and frequency that works best for you. This takes the guesswork out of saving and helps you stay on track with your goals. Plus, you won't even have to think about it once it's set up!

4. Invest in stocks, bonds, and other assets: Consider investing in a mix of stocks, bonds, and other assets to help grow your wealth over time. Consult a financial advisor or do your own research to determine the best investment options for your goals and risk tolerance. It's important to invest in a diverse mix of assets to help grow your wealth over time. Here are a few more tips to keep in mind when investing:

1. Diversify your portfolio: Don't put all your eggs in one basket. Diversify your investments across different asset classes, sectors, and geographic regions to help reduce risk.
2. Consider your risk tolerance: Your risk tolerance will affect the types of investments you choose. If you're risk-averse, you may want to consider more conservative investments, such as bonds or index funds. If you're comfortable with risk, you may want to consider more aggressive investments, such as individual stocks or actively managed funds.
3. Keep an eye on fees: Fees can eat into your investment returns over time. Look for low-cost investment options, such as index funds or ETFs, and avoid high-fee actively managed funds.
4. Stay disciplined: Don't let short-term market fluctuations or emotional reactions derail your long-term investment strategy. Stick to your investment plan and focus on your long-term goals.

5. Diversify your portfolio: Spread your investments across different asset classes, industries, and regions to reduce your risk and increase your potential returns. Diversification is an important strategy for managing risk and maximizing returns in your investment portfolio. By investing in a variety of assets such as stocks, bonds, and real estate, you can spread your risk and reduce the impact of market fluctuations on your overall portfolio. It's important to note that diversification does not guarantee a profit or protect against the loss, but it can help minimize the impact of volatility in the markets. Additionally, it's important to periodically review and rebalance your portfolio to ensure that it continues to align with your investment goals and risk tolerance.

6. Stay disciplined: Avoid making impulsive investment decisions based on emotions or short-term market fluctuations. Stick to your investment plan and stay disciplined to achieve your long-term financial goals. Sticking to your investment plan is key to achieving your long-term financial goals. It's important to remember that investing is a long-term game, and short-term fluctuations in the market should not deter you from your goals.

Instead of trying to time the market or make impulsive decisions, focus on building a diversified portfolio that aligns with your goals and risk tolerance, and stay disciplined by regularly reviewing and rebalancing your investments as needed.

Building Good Habits

Here we will discuss the importance of building good financial habits, such as avoiding debt, living below one's means, and avoiding impulse purchases. Provide tips for staying motivated and disciplined in the pursuit of financial freedom. Building good financial habits is crucial for achieving and maintaining financial freedom. Here are some tips for developing positive financial habits:

1. Avoid debt
2. Live below your means
3. Avoid impulse purchases
4. Automate your finances.
5. Track your progress
6. Stay disciplined

By developing positive financial habits and staying disciplined, you can achieve financial freedom and enjoy a more secure financial future.

1. **Avoid debt**: It's important to avoid taking on debt whenever possible, an especially high-interest debt like credit card debt. If you do have debt, prioritize paying it off as quickly as possible. High-interest debt can quickly accumulate and become a burden on your finances, making it difficult to achieve financial freedom.

To avoid debt, it's important to live below your means and avoid overspending. This may involve creating a budget and sticking to it, avoiding impulse purchases, and finding ways to reduce your expenses. It can also be helpful to establish an emergency fund to cover unexpected expenses, so you don't have to rely on credit cards or loans.

2. **Live below your means**: It's easy to get caught up in a cycle of spending more than you make. Instead, focus on living below your means by creating a budget and sticking to it. This can help you avoid overspending and keep your finances in check. Here are some more tips to live below your means:

- Cut back on unnecessary expenses: Take a close look at your budget and identify areas where you can cut back on expenses. This might include eating out less, canceling subscriptions you don't use, or finding cheaper alternatives to your regular purchases.

- Avoid lifestyle inflation: As your income increases, it's important to resist the temptation to increase your spending at the same rate. Instead, try to maintain your current lifestyle and put the extra money towards your financial goals.

- Delay gratification: It can be tempting to make impulse purchases or indulge in things you can't afford, but it's important to learn to delay gratification. Consider waiting a day or two before making a purchase to see if you really need it or if it fits into your budget.

- Practice mindful spending: When you do spend money, make sure it aligns with your values and priorities. Ask yourself if the purchase will bring long-term value or if it's just a short-term pleasure.

3. **Avoid impulse purchases**: Before making a purchase, take some time to consider whether it's something you really need or want. Avoid impulse purchases by creating a list of things you need and sticking to them. Additionally, try to wait a few days before making any non-essential purchases.

This can help you avoid impulse buying and give you time to think about whether the purchase is really worth it. You might also consider setting a spending limit for non-essential purchases each month and sticking to it. This can help you prioritize your spending and avoid overspending on things that don't align with your long-term financial goals.

4. **Automate your finances**: Automating your finances can help you stay on track with your financial goals. Set up automatic bill payments, savings transfers, and debt payments to make sure you never miss a payment and are always making progress toward your goals. Automating your finances can be a great way to stay on top of your finances and achieve your financial goals. By setting up automatic bill payments, savings transfers, and debt payments, you can ensure that you never miss a payment or fall behind on your financial obligations.

Here are some tips for automating your finances:

1. Set up automatic bill payments: Many banks and credit card companies offer the option to set up automatic bill payments. This allows you to pay your bills on time each month without having to worry about forgetting or missing a payment.

2. Set up automatic savings transfers: You can also set up automatic transfers from your checking account to your savings account. This ensures that you are consistently saving money and making progress toward your financial goals.

3. Set up automatic debt payments: If you have debt, such as a mortgage, car loan, or student loan, you can set up automatic payments to ensure that you are always making your payments on time.

4. Monitor your accounts: While automation can be helpful, it's still important to monitor your accounts regularly to make sure that everything is running smoothly. Check your account balances, review your transactions, and make any necessary adjustments to your automated payments or transfers.

5. **Track your progress**: Keeping track of your finances and monitoring your progress can help keep you motivated and on track. Use a budgeting app or spreadsheet to keep track of your income, expenses, and savings. Tracking your progress is essential in achieving your financial goals. You can keep a record of your expenses, income, and savings. This can help you see where you can cut back on spending and identify areas where you can save more. It can also help you stay motivated by seeing your progress over time.

Additionally, tracking your investments and their performance can help you make informed decisions about your portfolio and adjust your strategy as needed. Additionally, it's important to regularly review your financial goals and track your progress toward achieving them. This will help you stay motivated and make any necessary adjustments to your spending or saving habits. Celebrate your successes and learn from your mistakes to continue improving your financial situation.

6. **Stay disciplined**: Developing good financial habits takes time and discipline. Stay motivated by reminding yourself of your financial goals and celebrating small victories along the way. Yes, that's right! Staying disciplined is crucial when it comes to building good financial habits. It's important to stay focused on your long-term goals and avoid getting sidetracked by short-term distractions. Here are a few tips for staying motivated and disciplined:

1. Set clear goals: Write down your financial goals and keep them in a visible place where you can see them every day. This will remind you of why you're working so hard to build good habits and help keep you motivated.

2. Break your goals into smaller milestones: Instead of focusing on your long-term goals, break them down into smaller, achievable milestones. Celebrate each milestone along the way to keep yourself motivated.

3. Create a support system: Surround yourself with people who support your goals and can help hold you accountable. This could be friends, family, or even a financial advisor.

4. Focus on the benefits: Instead of focusing on the sacrifices you're making to build good habits, focus on the benefits you'll enjoy in the future. This could be things like financial freedom, peace of mind, and the ability to pursue your passions without worrying about money.

5. Practice self-discipline: Building good financial habits requires self-discipline. Practice saying no to impulse purchases, sticking to your budget, and avoiding debt. Over time, these habits will become second nature and help you achieve your financial goals.

Overcoming Obstacles

Acknowledge the obstacles that can prevent people from achieving financial freedom, such as lack of discipline, unexpected expenses, and economic downturns. Here is guidance on how to stay on track despite these obstacles. Financial freedom is a worthy goal, but it's not always easy to achieve. There are many obstacles that can get in the way, including lack of discipline, unexpected expenses, and economic downturns. Here are some tips on how to stay on track despite these obstacles:

1. Lack of Discipline
2. Unexpected Expenses
3. Economic Downturns
4. Lack of Knowledge

Remember, achieving financial freedom is a journey, not a destination. Stay motivated and committed to your goals, and don't let obstacles discourage you. With discipline, preparation, and a little bit of luck, you can overcome any obstacle and achieve financial freedom.

1. **Lack of Discipline**: Discipline is key to achieving financial freedom. It can be difficult to stay disciplined, especially when you're tempted to make impulsive purchases or skip saving for the month. To combat this, try setting specific financial goals and creating a plan to achieve them. Then, hold yourself accountable by tracking your progress and celebrating small victories along the way.

In addition, it can be helpful to automate your finances by setting up automatic transfers for savings, bills, and debt payments. This can take decision-making out of the equation and make it easier to stay on track. Additionally, consider finding an accountability partner or joining a support group to help you stay motivated and on track with your financial goals.

Finally, remember that building good financial habits takes time and effort, so don't get discouraged if you slip up. Instead, use any mistakes as an opportunity to learn and improve your habits going forward.

2. **Unexpected Expenses**: Unexpected expenses, such as medical bills or car repairs, can throw a wrench in your financial plans.

To prepare for these expenses, make sure you have an emergency fund with at least three to six months' worth of living expenses. Also, consider purchasing insurance policies, such as health or car insurance, to help mitigate the financial impact of unexpected events. Having insurance policies in place is a smart way to protect your finances from unexpected expenses. Additionally, it's a good idea to regularly review your budget and look for areas where you can cut back on expenses to free up some extra cash in case of emergencies.

Finally, if unexpected expenses do arise, try to avoid taking on high-interest debt to cover them. Instead, look for ways to generate extra income or consider alternative financing options, such as a personal loan with a lower interest rate.

3. **Economic Downturns**: Economic downturns, such as recessions or job losses, can be challenging for anyone. To protect yourself, consider diversifying your investments and creating a financial plan that includes contingencies for economic downturns. This may include setting aside additional savings or reducing your expenses to help weather any financial storms. Also, it's important to stay calm and avoid making impulsive decisions during economic downturns. Don't panic and sell your investments out of fear, as this can result in significant losses. Instead, work with a financial advisor to develop a long-term investment strategy that takes into account economic cycles and volatility. Finally, consider acquiring new skills or furthering your education to make yourself more employable in a changing job market.

4. **Lack of Knowledge**: Many people struggle with financial management because they lack knowledge or experience in this area. To overcome this obstacle, consider taking courses or reading books on personal finance to help improve your financial literacy. You may also consider consulting a financial advisor to help guide you through the process.

There are many resources available to help improve your financial knowledge and literacy. In addition to taking courses or reading books, you can also attend workshops or seminars, listen to podcasts, or follow personal finance blogs and websites. It's important to continuously educate yourself and stay up-to-date on the latest financial news and trends to make informed decisions about your money.

Conclusion

Now I will summarize the key points of the book and encourage people to take action toward achieving financial freedom. In summary, achieving financial freedom requires building good habits, making wise investment decisions, staying disciplined, and overcoming obstacles such as lack of discipline, unexpected expenses, economic downturns, and lack of knowledge.

By avoiding debt, living below your means, avoiding impulse purchases, automating your finances, diversifying your investments, tracking your progress, and seeking help when needed, you can move closer to your financial goals.

Remember to stay motivated and celebrate small victories along the way. The road to financial freedom may be challenging, but the rewards are well worth it. Take action today and start working towards achieving financial freedom.